FIRST LOVE

An Anthology

Drawings by Vivienne Flesher
Edited by Roy Finamore

STEWART, TABORI & CHANG
NEW YORK

"Girls We Have Known" is from the play of the same name, originally published by
Dramatists Play Service (© 1984, 1981 Ralph Pape); "Lovers" is reprinted by per-
mission of Georges Bourchardt, Inc. and the author (© 1973 by Russell Edson);
"Poison" originally appeared in *Haunts*, published by Cleveland State University
Press (© 1985 David Baker). "The Beginner's Book of Dreams" is from a work-in-
progress, to be published in 1987 by Alfred A. Knopf (© 1985 Elizabeth Benedict).

Published by Stewart, Tabori & Chang, Inc.
740 Broadway, New York, New York 10003

Library of Congress Cataloging-in-Publication Data
Main entry under title:

First love.
    1. American literature—20th century. 2. Love—Literary collections. I. Flesher,
Vivienne. II. Finamore, Roy.
PS509.L68F57   1986   810'.8'0354   85-27772
ISBN 0-941434-79-6

86 87 88 89 10 9 8 7 6 5 4 3 2 1

Distributed by Workman Publishing
1 West 39 Street, New York, New York 10018

Printed in the United States

First Edition

Contents

Foreword

The collection that follows is a garland of small pieces—what writers think when asked about first love—and it has been (as any anthology must be) a pleasure and a joy for the anthologist. So much of the pleasure has come from the writers themselves, from their enthusiasm, their open-handedness and open-heartedness, their kindness. The joy is here for all to see; it is on the page, from Shelby Moorman Howatt's ecstasy in discovering her own imagination to Marylin Butler's poignant outcry.

This is not, however, the place for someone to jump in and point out the good parts. They are here for you to read, to enjoy. The discovery of new doorways, the promise of the future, the unexpected glimpse of oneself, the curious ache of loss and its companion, freedom, the twinges and clumsiness and rapture and dizziness, the sense of adventure and at times of regret—these have all come at some time into our own lives. These, and more.

Each writer has packed a good deal of feeling into each short piece. Throughout runs a string of warmth, of the writer's strong feelings. In times that might almost be called foolish—often harsh, certainly confusing—what more could we ask for?

ROY FINAMORE

To Be Continued

The summer I'm four, my grandmother soaks my filthy fingernails in laundry bleach, clacking her teeth like a rattlesnake. But she rarely catches me. All she can see of me outside her kitchen window most days is a muddy foot sticking through the branches of my magic bush. She is bewildered by the ferocity that drives and keeps me hidden there. And of course, I can't explain. I have no words for the roar of blood in my head, the fever that liquefies my muscles in that green-gold kingdom under the bush.

"You're not yourself," Grandmother clacks when she can pin me down. She's right, but it's dangerous to tell her so. What would she do if she guessed that beneath the drooping branches I grow thunderbolt hair and lightning-bolt whiskers? While the soup cools, Grandmother talks and talks to the God whose picture is in our family Bible. He is everywhere, she says. Still, I know she would not be pleased to find Him quite so close to her kitchen door. The thought creates pleasant shivers in my stomach.

God's adventures unscroll faster than I

can fashion the stage settings. A battle between an ant and a dazed beetle requires a hastily built twig bridge over a puddle lake to accommodate the subplot—an ant's ladylove sailing beneath the fight on a leaf boat. A storm? Yes! God blows, lightning crackling from His whiskers, and then rescues all three players at the last minute. Troops from a neighboring anthill swarm to the scene. Sometimes, I'm an ant, too, scuttling with a thousand friends. Sometimes, being an ant makes me feel dizzy. I hug myself tightly, as my world goes 'round and 'round.

GLORIA GOLDREICH
Library

It was a small, narrow-windowed building, its red brick façade faded to a warm ochre color and its front door fashioned of gleaming oak and studded with polished brass hinges and an imposing plaque that read "Brooklyn Pvblic Library: Sheepshead Bay Branch." That angular "u" intrigued me. I pushed the door open and entered, walking on tiptoe lest the taps on the heels of my school shoes disturb the readers who sat at the long tables or stood before the

serried rows of books. I smiled, pleased to be back in my own magic kingdom with its various and wondrous fiefdoms—fiction and history, biography and poetry, the mysterious domains of astronomy and geography and the separate reference territory where dictionaries and atlases proudly rested on their dark walnut podiums.

I breathed in the mingled aromas of the room—the scent of paper and ink, of binding glue and wax, the slightly sour odor of earnest concentration and the miasmic fragrance of dreams and fantasies. The library sounds wafted about me in muted softness. Here, people whispered or spoke in the subdued tones of clandestine lovers; here, gestures substituted for words and smiles signified recognition.

At the front desk, my mouth dry and my hands shaking, I handed the bespectacled librarian the printed form signed by my father testifying that I was nine years old and he would be responsible for any debts I might incur. She read it carefully, gravely, aware that we were negotiating a serious and loving commitment. Finally, she reached for an oatmeal-colored piece of cardboard and handed it to me. My heart soared! At last, the gates of heaven swung open and I had my own library card.

I handled it tenderly, carefully, as all talismans of love must be handled as I moved through that room, reading titles and authors with a secret satisfaction. Mystery awaited me on those shelves, and beauty and knowledge. Older readers glanced at me and smiled in recognition. I was a new member of an old fraternity, a new initiate into an ancient and loving order.

My first selections of course were from the children's room—*The Blue Fairy Book* (oddly bound in red buckram), *An Old Fashioned Girl*, Helen Keller's *My Life*. The books were heavy in my arms as I left but my steps were light. I walked with the assurance of all lovers who are certain of the joy and permanence of their love—who know that each meeting will be followed by another and yet another in an infinity of wonder and discovery. My first love—that book-filled room, those quiet corridors—did not betray me. It gave me the secret of all my other loves, the knowledge that I might lose myself and gain unfathomable worlds.

DAVID W. DUNLAP
No Other Place

Purple snowflakes melt on the golden skin of Prometheus as he glides through Manhattan twilight. Uncountable forms pour from 70 floors of Radio Corporation, leaving their pinpoint signatures blazing above.

They don't see the 9-year-old frozen among their currents, terrified, enchanted. They don't know that he is hearing for the first time their city's awful claim: *I* am teacher in every art, *I* brought the fire.

From beneath the glass vaults of Pennsylvania Station, a streamline called the Broadway Limited carries him home. He burns in his berth under the mint-blue night light, unable to forget that he briefly spied the center of the universe.

And he will return to Manhattan one day, not because he wants to, but because he remembers that there is no other place.

JOHN CALVIN BATCHELOR
My First Love

I loved baseball before I knew what love is. Now that I know what love can be and should be, I also know that baseball has my heart forever.

I was spellbound by the magical domain of the game. I started playing little league at seven years old, and understood immediately that once I stepped into that holy diamond, the world of adults and school was outside, and only romance was inside. I know now that it is possible to love another inside that same sort of fabulous construction, so that the world is outside and only passion is inside, but no human being could ever be as giving and forgiving as home plate.

There was also my physical love of the game. I only had to throw hard and hear the whap of the ball striking the catcher's mitt to know that all was well. More, the excitement of a ground ball coming at me was worth all the waiting. And then there was hitting—the joy of feeling the bat when I hit the ball on the sweet spot, and it rocketed.

I did not play baseball after 12. Then came football and grammar, high school and girls. I am only a fan of the game now, and I do not really want to pitch for the Yankees or hit the long ball for L.A. I only want to hold onto my first love, and remember how it feels to be so intensely, so wildly, so bottomlessly happy.

REBECCA GOLDSTEIN
The Boarder

My impression was that we bought her together with the house. She was very old—for her hair was gray.

The house—dark and gloomy as it was—was special because it contained her. To enter that small front bedroom was to enter a world made magic by her strangeness. It even smelled different—a blend of Chiclets and cigarettes.

It was there that I came running with the great news the day we came home with my new sister, Sarah, three days after I myself turned three. And it was there that I retreated in the confusing weeks and months that followed, when my place in the household outside closed seamlessly over.

She saw me through other trying times as

18

well: the night our pediatrician came to dinner and I refused to go down—even though they assured me that he had left his hated black bag at home. She let me have my dinner in her room, and together we watched from the window for his departure.

She was a creature of rare fascination. But sometimes she scared me. That was when she would cough, unable to stop. "That's my smoker's cough," she'd say, when she finally caught her breath. "Promise me you'll never smoke."

She went away—they said to the hospital and I worried that she too would bring back a baby. Eventually my older sister moved into her room, and Sarah came in with me. But I could smell her Chiclets and cigarettes for a long time after.

T. R. PEARSON
Little Friend

I recollect the first one plain because she hid behind our pyracantha bush down at the ditch and looked at me, or anyhow looked up towards the house that I was in looking out at her. I was ten and so I'd had some considerable truck with girls, had tangled with any number of them and had got bit and gouged and sat on and one time had even got kicked in the stomach so hard that I had not figured I would ever again draw breath, but I'd never had one just look at me from behind a bush and not like she wanted to harm me even but like something else, like something else entirely. So I felt peculiar already when my momma found me at the window and laid her hand atop my head like she used to and said, "You've got a little friend outside." That made me feel more peculiar still and ashamed and embarrassed and just plain different, like I hadn't ever felt different before. And I told her, "I know," and put my nose to the glass.

DAVID BAKER
Poison

The summer Sally Millsap fell from the graceful
perch we shared on the split-rail fence
that divided bobbing necks of iris and jonquil
from the dusty, wilder ivy
we knew only to avoid, like the dead
animals we found in spring stinking up the
    cellar,

was the first time they tried to keep us apart.
That fast and she was gone, knees
kicked up and over, and me just laughing there
looking at her on the ground.

Her mother came flying at us from the house
and grabbed her up still breathless,
then looked at me hard. She was mad alright
and I felt my young skin grow
hot right there, and heard only a few words
as they trotted across the grass,
her mother saying *soap*, *soap*, saying *dirty girl*.

I played alone for days. Each morning my
    father
told me Sally was sick and I was one
lucky boy this time, and had to stay away.
So when I waited beneath her
window one afternoon, in a slow rain
that fell more like long hair, I was surprised
to see her up and walking in her room,

though when I tapped, and when she raised
the window, I finally saw
the price of our first sin. Her arms were
    chapped
red as burns, her eyes, even
in that dry house, wet as mine,

and when she smiled at me and spoke,
her whole face seemed swollen with the awful
   touch
our parents had told us once,
and would tell us so often after that, to avoid
no matter what it took.

ELIZABETH BENEDICT
The Beginners' Book of Dreams

It was like a dream. The way she was lying on
the opened-up Castro Convertible in the living
room under the covers long after everyone else
had gone upstairs to bed, thinking wouldn't it
be something if he came down here and
touched my leg the way he did today in the car,
wouldn't it be something if he gave me a kiss
on the lips at the same time as he touched my
leg, now that would be something.

   The way she was lying there in the dark
with her eyes closed, imagining a kiss, and she
heard the stairs creaking and thought he's coming to kiss me and thought no, I'm hearing
things, but oh, but what if I'm not, what will I
do, and she could feel her heart pound as she
was sure it would if he actually touched her,
and then he would know that she had never

kissed anyone because if she had her heart would not be pounding like this, if she had she would know exactly what to do when he kissed her, but what would probably happen, what would probably happen is that nothing would happen, he would just touch her leg again in the car on the way back to New York, if he had even touched it in the first place.

HOWARD SCHWARTZ
The Enchanted Mirror

There once was a king who married a princess from a distant kingdom. For three years they lived together in love, but then the queen became homesick for her native land. When the king learned of this he allowed her to take leave of him and journey home for a year. During her absence, however, the king did not care to rule his kingdom, and time after time his counselors failed to find a sorcerer who could be of help to him. Then one day an old beggar appeared at the palace and offered his services to the king. From his pocket he took two worn coins, coins in which the king's eyes saw the eyes of the queen looking up at him, and right then, without asking any questions, the king put down his crown and let the beggar become his guide.

Much to the king's surprise, the beggar did not lead him to a far corner of the kingdom, but to the royal forest on the southern side of the palace. Soon they reached a small clearing filled with the light of the setting sun. There the beggar rolled aside a log and revealed an underground entrance, and as soon as the king descended inside he heard the distant voice of his beloved singing, as she had often done while she wove in her room. The passage was barely large enough to proceed without difficulty, and the walls appeared to be mirrors, mirrors so dusty they only reflected the flame of his torch. If the king made a wrong turn the voice faded away, and thus he was guided through the labyrinth, the mirrors becoming clearer and clearer until at last he reached an enchanted mirror of dazzling brightness, where he saw the image of his wife reflected as clearly as if she stood there before him. For what seemed hours the king gazed upon his wife's features, basking in her presence and burning her image into his memory. Then he returned to the labyrinth, letting her voice lead him, and in a far shorter time than it had taken him to enter he found himself as-

cending the ladder to the clearing, and greeted the smiling face of the beggar once more. So too did he return to the labyrinth from time to time, to bask in the image of his beloved.

Now the queen had planned to return to the king at the end of the year, but in the ninth month of her absence she saw a young man as he walked past the garden outside her window, and she could not keep from falling in love with him. But because she was afraid to inform the king of her change of heart, the song that guided him through the labyrinth faded so gradually that he did not realize it until it had become no more than a whisper. And finally a night came when the king followed the almost imperceptible murmur to the end of the labyrinth only to discover that the mirror had grown dark, and though he tried to retrace his steps, he lost his way in the labyrinth that led him in loops and circles but gave him no hint of how to find the way out.

APRIL BERNARD
After Emily Dickinson

If there were just one Answer
to every Question posed,
If every thorn along the Way
bloomed—sudden—into Rose—

If blood be wet, and roses red,
and you—my Valentine—
Then does my heart await in me
as rubies—the pick—in mines?

ROSEMARY A. FOLEY
Eternal Love, Etc., Etc.

I fell in love with the back of his head, the
clerk/typist from Spiegel's Catalog. Too young
to work at fourteen, I became sixteen overnight
through the intercession of the 11th Ward
alderman. Spurred by my sudden maturity,
the novels of Colette and rampant hebephrenia
I ached to be ravished by this older clerk/typist
who was well into his twenties.

He ate alone and read Dos Passos. An
aisle separated us, and every day that summer
at work my hands imagined and my lips and

tongue pretended. I had made him the object of my very being and I dreamed of when, alone together, we'd be driven mad in a violent exchange of love and die in each other's arms.

By the end of July I still hadn't said hello. I had sent urgent telepathic messages to the back of his head. "Take me, please!" By the end of August I had started spying on him. After bumping into him several times he noticed me. One morning I collided into his coffee and he spoke. "That's all right, Jean, no harm done." He knew my name! Parts of my body, previously unfamiliar to me, engorged, sunk and liquefied. "Sorry," I choked and ran. I had to move fast. The following week I'd be back in boarding school.

By Friday I had developed a slight fever. After work that day I quickly trailed him out of the office and onto the 35th Street bus, hiding behind a flock of nuns. When he transferred to the Racine bus I transferred. At State & Monroe he got off and entered the Fair Store. I flitted from counter to pillar, keeping low but never losing sight of him. Up the escalator, past Shoes, Blouses, and into Lingerie.

I froze. Numbly, I stood and watched him buy a pair of scanty, red panties. "Why?" I shouted, not knowing what I was saying or

where I was. He spun around and blurted automatically, "For my wife. . . ."

"Why?" I cried, "why?"

"Be—because it's her birthday . . ." he stuttered, bewildered and embarrassed.

"You're married? You can't be! How could you do this to me?" I flew out of the store and wept so hard my face blew up and I never went back to work.

Now if I ever notice the back of some man's head I deliberately turn away and stare at the floor. Which is how I fell madly in love with this guy who wore sandals and read Ezra Pound's *Cantos*, etc., etc. . . .

RALPH PAPE
Girls We Have Known

ALAN. I used to fall in love all the time. I used to think it was love, anyway. Didn't take much, either. A smile, something about the eyes—

ERNIE. A flower in the hair?

ALAN. A flower in the hair, yeah. What the hell is that, anyway? That's not love. Although a lot of guys—

ERNIE. Richie Daly.

ALAN. Richie Daly. What did he always say about Marjorie? "I love her voice, I love her voice."

ERNIE. They're divorced.

ALAN. You can't fall in love with a voice. *(Pause.)* I've been seeing this woman for about six months. You've never met her or any-thing—

ERNIE. So?

ALAN. So I think maybe I'm in love with her.

ERNIE. You *think* you're in love with her? What's that supposed to mean?

ALAN. Boy, I don't know. You got me. I came across this old saying recently, to the effect that very few people would fall in love if they had never read about it. And I thought: God, that's so fucking depressing, it's probably true. But when I'm with this woman, Ernie, everything seems so *simple* and everything around us takes on such *clarity* that it seems beside the point whether you call it love or something else. And then I wonder if I'm worthy of it, of *her*, you know? That's the part that really scares me. *(Alan takes a drink and begins to recite, drama-tizing unconsciously.)* "So whoever loves must try to act as if he had a great work; he must be much alone and go into himself and collect himself and hold fast to himself; he must work;

he must become something!" Rilke said that. *(Pause.)*

ERNIE. Well, my friend, do you know what my advice to you is?

ALAN. What?

ERNIE. Don't think about it. *(Pause.)* Socrates said that.

ALAN. He did not.

ERNIE. Well. He meant to.

CATHERINE BUSH
Three Fries, Ten Burgers

I say our number is 18. Cal says it's 11. We're already in the line past the cashier. Three fries and ten hamburgers, flat little squares like stamps on mini buns, you know, not like anything else anywhere. You never listen to me, Cal says. The man ahead of us ordered a dozen to go. That's what makes it special at White Castle. The girl behind the wire grid flips these small squares in the white bright light. Blips of hunger or excitement start going off inside me. You never believe me, Cal says. The rows of tiny boxes rock me with amazement. Believe, I say, what's believe got to do with it?

I open up my boxes. Don't yell, Cal yells.
The burgers are the size of buttons. The french
fries are like toothpicks; the burgers are like
bottle caps. I pick one up. My fingertips tingle; my hands tingle. I swallow. Everything's
fizzing, all the way down my throat, all the
way down my arm to the tiny wooden prong.
Cal's yelling something else. He splats his
hand on the counter. I'm saying, you're crazy,
you're crazy. My fries are shrinking smaller
than threads; the hamburgers no bigger than
pills, than spores. My stomach pings and
aches. Things disappearing right before your
eyes, that's what love is. I know it's real because it hurts.

BARRY YOURGRAU
Earthquake

We've just met. We're in love, though we
shouldn't be. But we want to be. We sneak off
from work and steal upstairs to our rented
room. We pull back the quilt, hot from sunlight, and we embrace: the bed shakes, the
walls shake, the floor trembles back and forth.
We lounge back at last on the pillows; the bed
goes on shaking, the walls shudder, the wash

bowl rattles on its stand. "It's an earthquake!" you murmur. "Is that what we've done?" "Look at that!" I tell you. "The mirror's fallen to the floor but it hasn't broken at all!"

Afterwards, when things have quieted down, we try to straighten up the room. We hang the mirror back on its nail. But we're too excited to finish all of it. We hurry down to the front steps and sit there, holding hands and eating oranges and watching the city tidy up. Bells are ringing everywhere. Fire engines clang. We look on in delight as men with hearts on their helmets come running up, to where a big truck has turned over, spilling its cargo of love letters into the street.

RUSSELL EDSON
Lovers

There was a blind owl which was loved by a squirrel with a crushed head.

If the squirrel thought the owl was a squirrel, the owl thought the squirrel was an owl—Did it matter?—I mean, in the night, would it matter when the squirrel was upon its mate; the owl on her back pressing closer the squirrel with wings dormant for love . . .

And could it matter after the act when the great woman owl murmured, don't move, stay . . .

The squirrel is restless.

The owl sighing, don't move, honey . . .

The squirrel wants a drink of water, I'll be back in a minute . . .

Stay with me, honey . . .

Many nights of this.

EMILY PRAGER
A New Love

"'A new love,' she writes, 'is like a baby's face before age stretches it beyond recognition, and pockmarks of betrayal mar its puberty, and sags and lines and creases set its dotage.'"

"Good Christ, that's awfully cynical."

"Yes, well, of course she's still in the post-breakup stage. She doesn't believe she will ever love again."

"Oh, rot! It was the same thing last time and then we went to Jack's party—I'll never forget—I was standing right next to her as we entered the living room and suddenly I felt pinned in this field of electricity. I turned and

I swear she was taller and her breasts had grown two inches. She was staring at this lovely man—the recently departed Ben—and he at her, and all the pain and anguish of their ill-fused lives was blown out by the current running through them."

"I remember. That night she went home and repainted her apartment. She had her hair cut, bought all new underwear, and I didn't see her cry again for a year and a half. They were dangerous and adorable to be around, those two."

"Hmm, yes . . . a baby's face. A jolly, smiling baby's face. It was like that, in the beginning. I take it back. It really was. . . . Were we?"

"Of course."

"And now?"

". . . Grandma Moses."

"Oh . . . oh, okay, okay. I'll accept that."

DIANE ACKERMAN
The Upkeep of the Fire

Here's my best offer:
by nightfall, depth charges
under fluorescent seas,

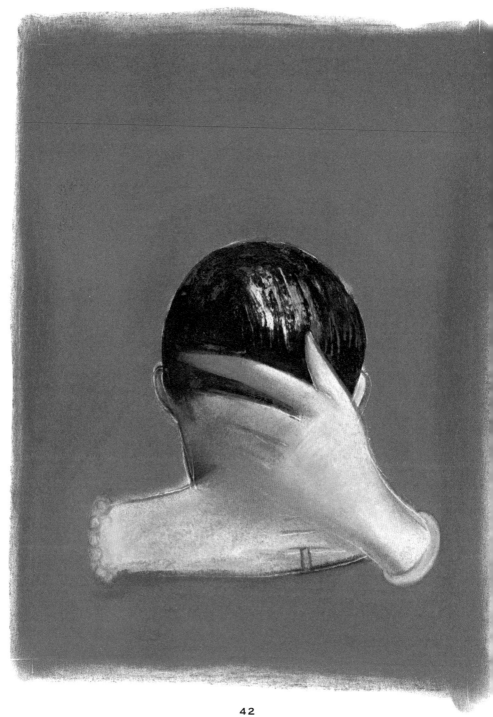

the known world remapped,
time tilted free
from the oarlocks of each day,
until we lose track
of infinity in a passing moment,
our flesh hot as oil lamps
swinging, swinging,
on an ocean-going vessel
whose scuttlebutt is passion.
On your chest, a tattoo
so blue your ribs quiver,
a tattoo I apply by hand;
it would last forever,
and contain all the constellations
in the many-sabled night.
Each time you opened your shirt
it would be there: the desert simooms,
the backbone of light,
the lost trade routes
to the edge of world and wit,
the sheer glitter on daring's catwalk.
I would teach you about
the Easter Island of the heart.
And you would pay without ceasing,
new hungers that dizzy
or unkennel me, spot-welds
that arc to the core of me.
And I would love you

in the clip-clop of life's
cobblestone, where draft horses
pull down streets
only a heartbeat wide, only you
in the minor miracles of light,
in the mirrored alleyways,
in the deathwatch of autumn
where, like two bat wings,
my dark eyes beat.

FREDERICK BUSCH
Mitzi

Mitzi was short, thin, pale, pretty. We were
five when we loved each other, and six when,
each day after school, we sat in her parents'
apartment on the corner of Avenue I and
Ocean Avenue. There was the big easy chair,
and there was her father on whose lap I sometimes sat—he was big and welcoming, like the
chair—and on their small, blue-flickering
DuMont we watched *Swiss Family Robinson*. I
came to love this program, then its source,
Robinson Crusoe, and later read it often. The
cave of dreamings constructed from that lap,
the fictive stranded family, and Mitzi Gropper
whom I loved: out of it all came fictions, and in

no small way *because* of it all. I still write of stranded people, alone and tempted by that solitude, yet knowing they must try to escape it. Mitzi did.

JILL MacNEICE
Ah, Nick . . .

Because you waited in the cold God knows how long for me behind the bush, the Burning Bush, as I've come to think of it, and grabbed me by the arm and held me so close I could smell the onion on your breath (the faint scent of onion on certain swarthy men still makes my knees go weak), and rubbed street ice in my face that burned so cold it brought tears to my eyes, and especially because my mother laughed when I came home crying and said it means he loves you, boys *will* be boys (I was desperate for a sign, scribbling your name, our names, TRUE LOVE ALWAYS, on my notebook) I believed you loved me, too. After all, didn't the girls cry when Georgie-Porgie kissed them? (Girls *are* always crying.) I've kissed a hundred since and cried my share, but no one's *ever* smashed me in the face like you.

MARK O'DONNELL
I Made Me Love You

I'm told that as a child I resisted chocolate ice cream, claiming it was vanilla ice cream that had gotten dirty, but of course I then ate it. When I entered puberty, I tried to fantasize about cleansingly blonde student council girls, but the yin hit the yang and my first passion was for a dark-haired, soft-eyed, surly delinquent who broke windows with his fists and dropped out of twelfth grade to take a job as a meat cutter. He'd been the Marlon Brando of our drama class, but was in fact a rebel, so couldn't be trusted with even the rebel parts.

I doubted myself, so prized association with his manly abandon, and imagined subsuming it—I became avid Smee to his broody Hook, hoping by tending his unrest to have both hearth and adventure, to cover all human bases at once. At my encouragement, he convinced me to go to a summer's acting school in New York City, a wild gambit for blue-collar Cleveland, where travel was considered presumptuous. My parents reluctantly allowed it; my mother asked what power he had over me, but neither of us wanted the answer. He and I eloped (to my mind) to Manhattan, my first plane ride and the first time I'd been separated from my large family and twin brother.

He only stayed for two weeks; he didn't like the teachers telling him what to do, and as I consider it now, perhaps he realized his roommate at the Y was tightening from friendship to fever. He left a note on his bed explaining he was leaving the dirty hustle for cousins in West Virginia. My tuition money had been hard-earned, so I was allowed to remain for the rest of the summer, wandering the streets deifically, assimilating all the fantastic episodes and characters, alone. It was my introduction to that other adult prerogative, self-structured privacy. Unwillingly, I tasted love's tonic antidote, freedom.

ROBERT OLEN BUTLER
Another Country

She explained how in her country a child would put tree sap on the end of a bamboo pole and reach up and catch a cicada and keep it in her room to hear it sing. Its song, made private for her, would bring good luck all her life. And when the hot Asian wind blew, the silk panels of her *ao dai* thrashed in the sunlight

like his happiness at being with her thrashed in the center of his chest.

But then he was short of time in her country and he was also short of breath and he was short of any feelings at all except a fear that his own good luck would run out and he would die only a handful of days before going home. It was she who wept when he left.

Six years later, as he sat before a TV in a dark room, he saw the last choppers hammering away from the embassy roof. And then he wept.

MARYLIN BUTLER
I Love You

I want to show you
the maple leaves
growing. I want
to be there and watch
your eyes wake
as the time
cleaves and you can see
through it: two winged seeds,
the young leaves.

I want to hear you

speak for hours about
the world beginning,
about dust pollen and
time's insane ashes,
bloodroots and promises.

I won't be visible,
if you prefer.
I can avoid
presences and words.
I can walk in shades
that don't reflect color.
I can be a person
of no body or mind.

We can meet in
solitude.
You don't even
have to remember.

DESIGN

J.C. Suares

Kathleen Gates

Andrea Perrine

PRODUCTION

Katherine van Kessel

Printed and bound in the United States